Handwriting Practice Workbook for Adults

Children's Reading & Writing Education Books

All Rights reserved. No part of this book may be reproduced or used in any way or form or by any means whether electronic or mechanical, this means that you cannot record or photocopy any material ideas or tips that are provided in this book

Copyright 2016

Trace and rewrite
the famous quotes.

Life is really simple,
but we insist on
making it complicated.
—Confucius

It is often in the darkest skies that we see the brightest stars.
—Richard Paul Evans

Life is like a box of chocolates. You never know what you're going to get.
—Forrest Gump

Where there is love there is life.
     —Mahatma Ghandi

Most people do not listen with the intent to understand; they listen with the intent to reply.
—Stephen R. Covey

Go confidently in the direction of your dreams! Live the life you've imagined.
—Henry David Thoreau

I only regret that I have but one life to give for my country.
—Nathan Hale

Life is either a daring adventure or nothing at all.
—Helen Keller

In three words I can
sum up everything
I've learned about
life: It goes on.
                    —Robert Frost

Only a life lived for others is a life worthwhile.
— Albert Einstein

The greatest glory in living lies not in never falling, but in rising every time we fall.
—Nelson Mandela

In this life we cannot do great things. We can only do small things with great love.
—Mother Teresa

As is our confidence,
so is our capacity.
—William Hazlitt

Others have seen what is and asked why. I have seen what could be and asked why not.
—Pablo Picasso

Love all, trust a few,
do wrong to none.
 —William Shakespeare

It does not matter how slowly you go as long as you do not stop.
— Confucius

Nature does not hurry, yet everything is accomplished.

—Lao Tzu

Health is the greatest gift, contentment the greatest wealth, faithfulness the best relationship.
　　　　　　　　—Buddha

The only impossible journey is the one you never begin.
—Anthony Robbins

*Life is ours to be spent,
not to be saved.
—D. H. Lawrence*

Love the life
you live.
Live the life
you love.
—Bob Marley

All that we see and seem is but a dream within a dream.

—Edgar Allan Poe

Do not let making a living prevent you from making a life.
—John Wooden

Never let the fear
of striking out keep
you from playing
the game.
—Babe Ruth

Everything has beauty, but not everyone sees it.
—Confucius

You will face many defeats in life, but never let yourself be defeated.
—Maya Angelou

No act of kindness, no matter how small, is ever wasted.

—Aesop

In order to write
about life first you
must live it.
—Ernest Hemingway

Live in the sunshine,
swim the sea, drink
the wild air.
    —Ralph Waldo Emerson

*When you realize
nothing is lacking,
the whole world
belongs to you.*

—Lao Tzu

The only person
you are destined to
become is the person
you decide to be.
    —Ralph Waldo Emerson

Life is never fair, and perhaps it is a good thing for most of us that it is not.
—Oscar Wilde

Life's tragedy is that we get old too soon and wise too late.
—Benjamin Franklin

If life were predictable it would cease to be life, and be without flavor.
—Eleanor Roosevelt

In the end, it's not the years in your life that count. It's the life in your years.
—Abraham Lincoln

Choose a job you love, and you will never have to work a day in your life.
—Confucius

www.ingramcontent.com/pod-product-compliance
Lightning Source LLC
LaVergne TN
LVHW082253070426
835507LV00034B/2276